Highlights

창의력 쑥쑥 숨은그림찾기™
Hidden Pictures™

표지 그림 _ R. 마이클 팰런 R. Michael Palan

Christmas tree ornament
크리스마스 트리 장식품

boomerang
부메랑

top hat
남성용 정장 모자

cane
지팡이

baseball bat
야구방망이

T-shirt
티셔츠

needle
바늘

ice-cream bar
막대아이스크림

tube of toothpaste
치약튜브

banana
바나나

saltshaker
소금 뿌리개

2 rabbits
토끼 두 마리

fish
물고기

drinking straw
빨대

Highlights

button
단추

pencil
연필

recorder
리코더

mitten
벙어리장갑

spoon
숟가락

bell
종

crescent
moon
초승달

iron
다리미

slice of pizza
피자 조각

squirrel
다람쥐

snake
뱀

envelope
봉투

open book
펴놓은 책

turtle
거북

lollipop
막대사탕

Illustrated by Karen Stormer Brooks

ruler
자

key
열쇠

light bulb
백열전구

magnet
자석

olive
올리브

slice of pie
파이 조각

fish
물고기

pocket watch
회중시계

Illustrated by Diana Zourelias

heart
하트

needle
바늘

snail
달팽이

flashlight
손전등

bell
종

acorn
도토리

lollipop
막대사탕

caterpillar
애벌레

ring
반지

hot dog
핫도그

saucepan
냄비

paper clip
클립

slice of toast
토스트 조각

Highlights

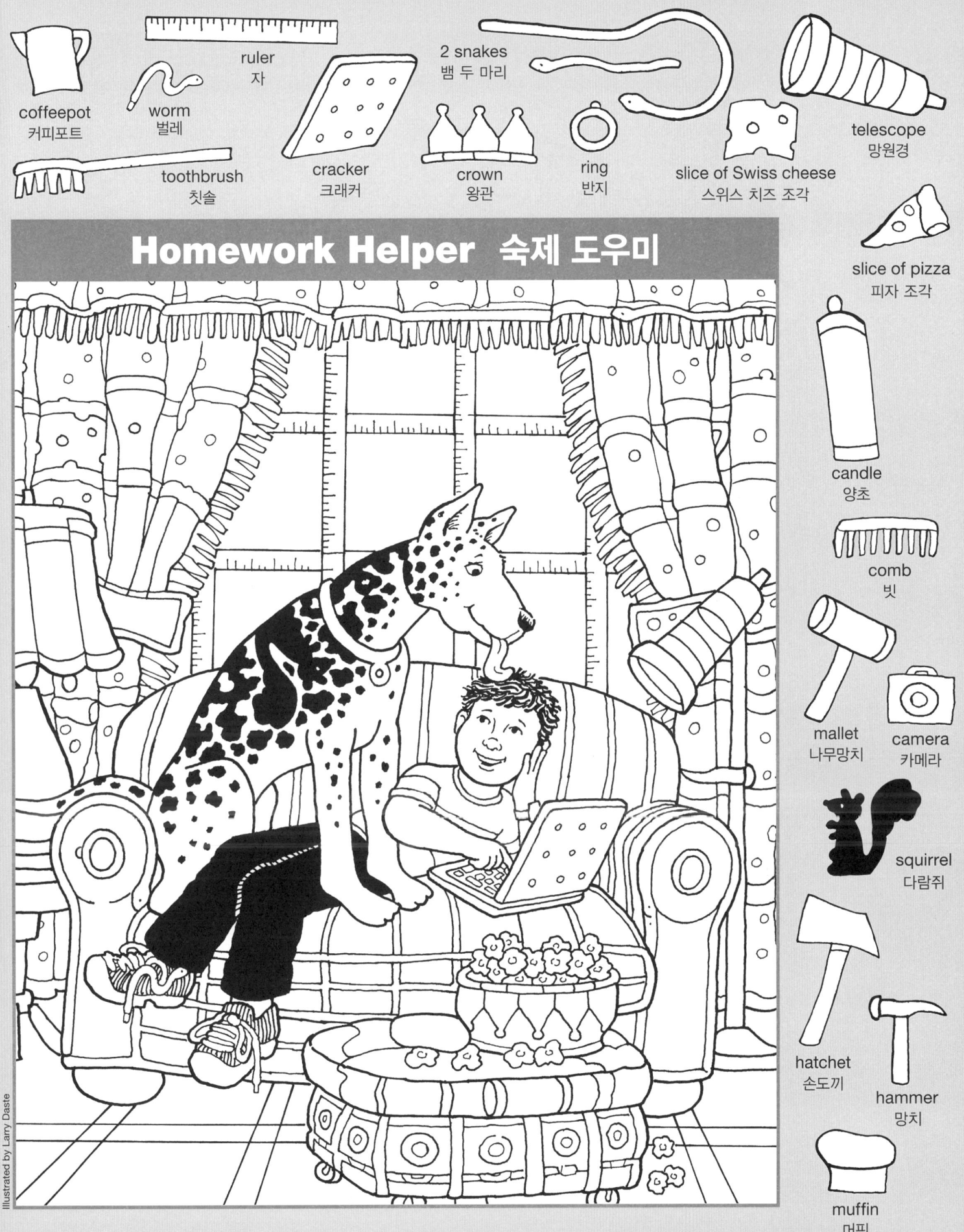

coffeepot
커피포트

worm
벌레

ruler
자

toothbrush
칫솔

cracker
크래커

2 snakes
뱀 두 마리

crown
왕관

ring
반지

slice of Swiss cheese
스위스 치즈 조각

telescope
망원경

slice of pizza
피자 조각

candle
양초

comb
빗

mallet
나무망치

camera
카메라

squirrel
다람쥐

hatchet
손도끼

hammer
망치

muffin
머핀

Homework Helper 숙제 도우미

Illustrated by Larry Daste

Highlights **5**

button
단추

paintbrush
페인트붓

nail
못

baseball
bat
야구방망이

candle
양초

sailboat
돛단배

ruler
자

lollipop
막대사탕

spoon
숟가락

tack
압정

pencil
연필

envelope
봉투

snake
뱀

Highlights

bird
새

artist's brush
그림붓

eyeglasses
안경

slice of pie
파이 조각

toothbrush
칫솔

rabbit
토끼

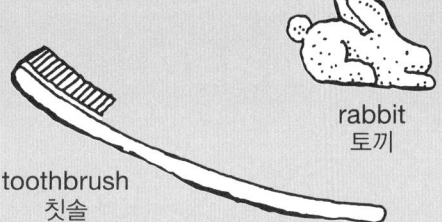

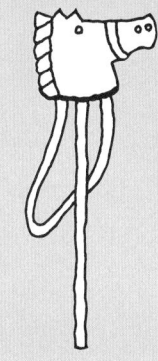
hobby horse
장난감 목마

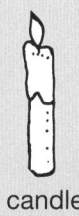
candle
양초

spoon
숟가락

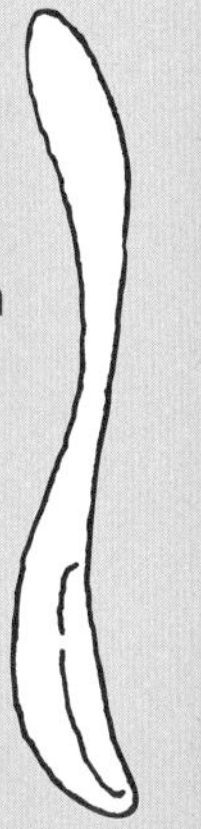

hammer
망치

bow
나비 모양의
리본

golf club
골프채

Sidewalk Skateboarders 인도에서 스케이트보드 타기

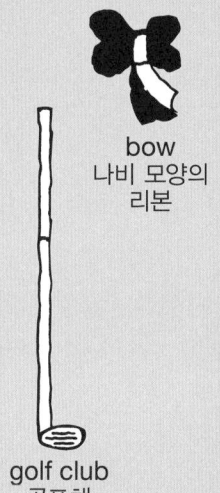

Illustrated by R. Michael Palan

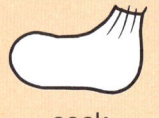

sock
양말

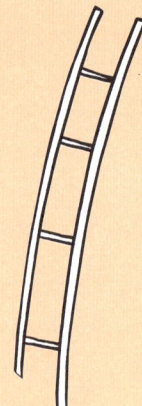

ladder
사다리

celery
셀러리

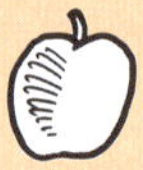

apple
사과

party hat
파티 모자

telephone
receiver
전화 수화기

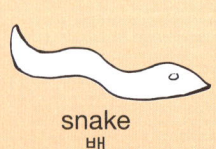

snake
뱀

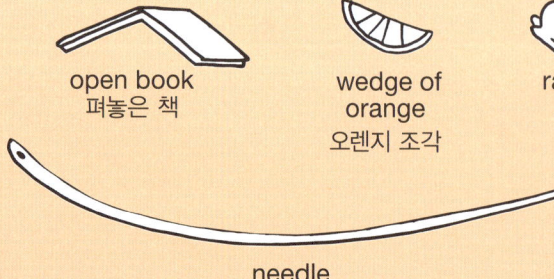

open book
펴놓은 책

wedge of
orange
오렌지 조각

rabbit
토끼

horseshoe
편자(말발굽에 붙이는 쇳조각)

banana
바나나

spoon
숟가락

needle
바늘

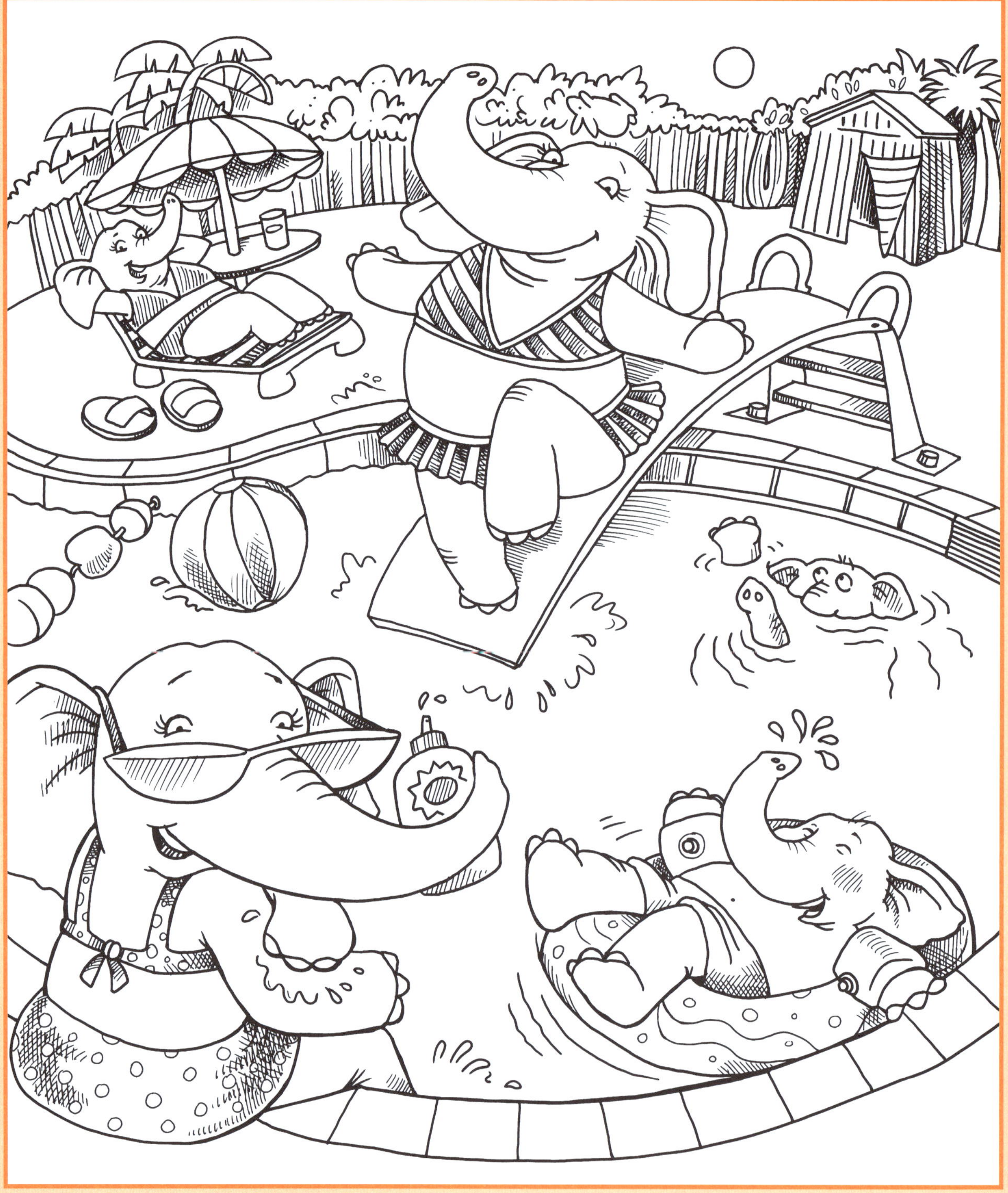

Illustrated by Karen Stormer Brooks

feather
깃털

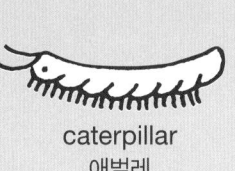
caterpillar
애벌레

boot
부츠

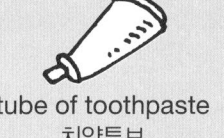
tube of toothpaste
치약튜브

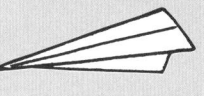
paper airplane
종이비행기

drinking straw
빨대

A Stroll in the Park 즐거운 공원 산책

wristwatch
손목시계

canoe
카누

ice-cream
cone
아이스크림 콘

clothespin
빨래집게

candy cane
크리스마스용 가락엿

bowl
그릇

seashell
조개껍질

Illustrated by Ron Leiser

 9

Who, Me? 누구, 나?

teacup
찻잔

wishbone
V자형 뼈

peanut
땅콩

chili pepper
칠리 페퍼
(매운 맛이 강한
칠레 고추)

apple core
사과 속

acorn
도토리

lollipop
막대사탕

banana
바나나

pretzel
프레첼
(매듭 모양의 과자)

doughnut
도넛

slice of bread
빵 조각

olive
올리브

grapes
포도

carrot
당근

10 Highlights

Illustrated by Rocky Fuller

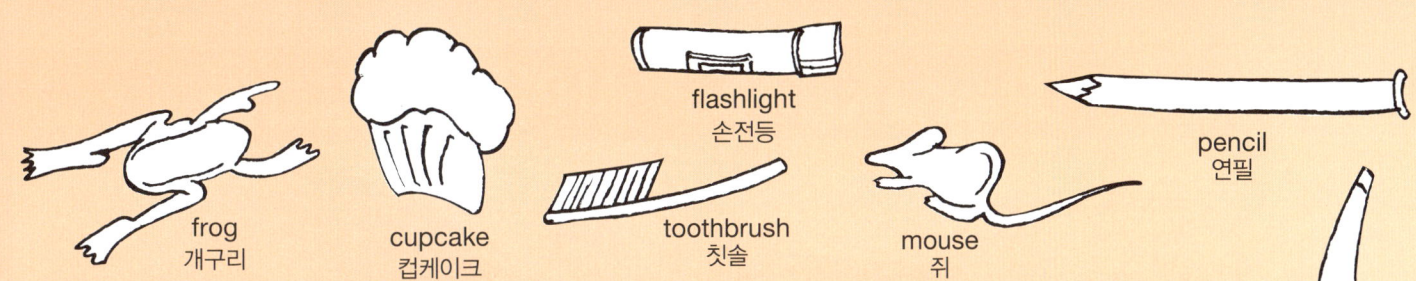

frog
개구리

cupcake
컵케이크

flashlight
손전등

toothbrush
칫솔

mouse
쥐

pencil
연필

Sailing with Dad   아빠와 함께하는 신나는 뱃놀이

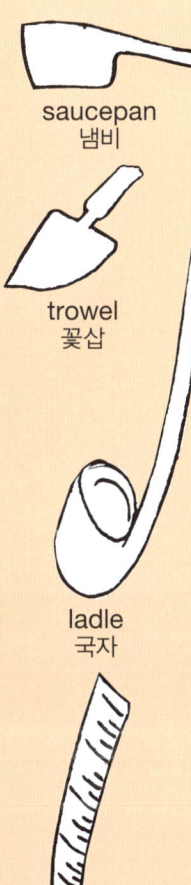

banana
바나나

saucepan
냄비

trowel
꽃삽

ladle
국자

ruler
자

pear
배

apple
사과

rabbit
토끼

Illustrated by Chuck Galey

Parakeets 사이좋은 잉꼬들

tiger's head
호랑이의 머리

turtle
거북

mouse
쥐

ice-cream cone
아이스크림 콘

candy cane
크리스마스용 가락엿

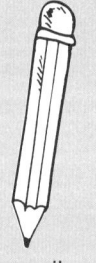

pencil
연필

gingerbread
man
생강 쿠키

sailboat
돛단배

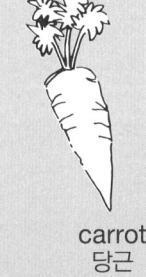

carrot
당근

needle
바늘

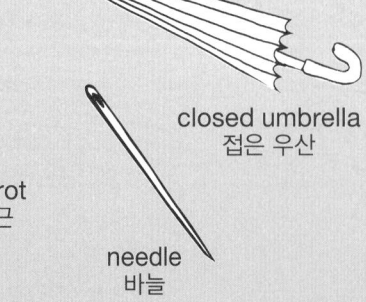

closed umbrella
접은 우산

snake
뱀

fish
물고기

handbag
핸드백

chili pepper
칠리 페퍼

Highlights

Illustrated by Susan T. Hall

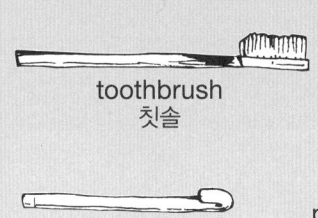
toothbrush
칫솔

cane
지팡이

paper airplane
종이비행기

fish
물고기

cupcake
컵케이크

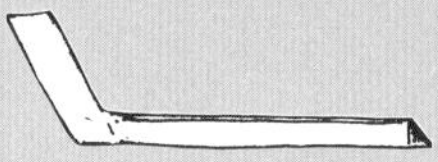

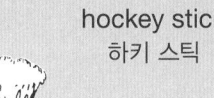
hockey stick
하키 스틱

spoon
숟가락

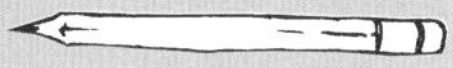

pencil
연필

football
럭비공

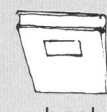
book
책

Giddyup! 이랴!

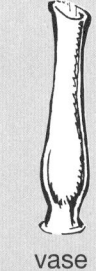

vase
꽃병

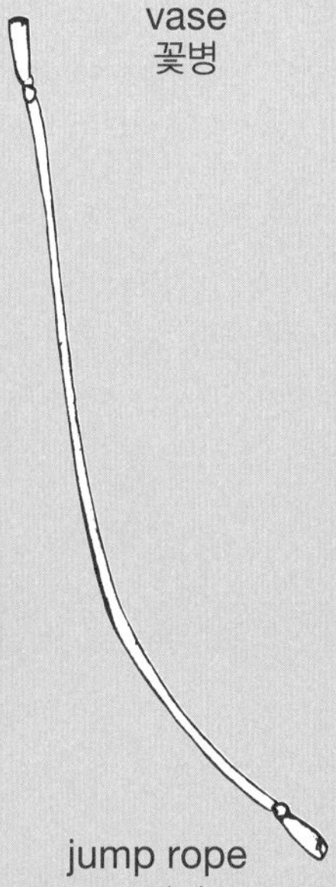

jump rope
줄넘기

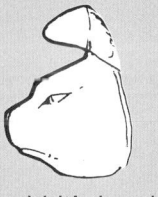
rabbit's head
토끼의 머리

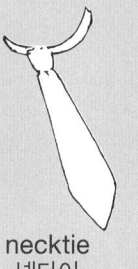
necktie
넥타이

Illustrated by Patrick Coleman

Howdy, Neighbor! 옆집 친구야, 안녕!

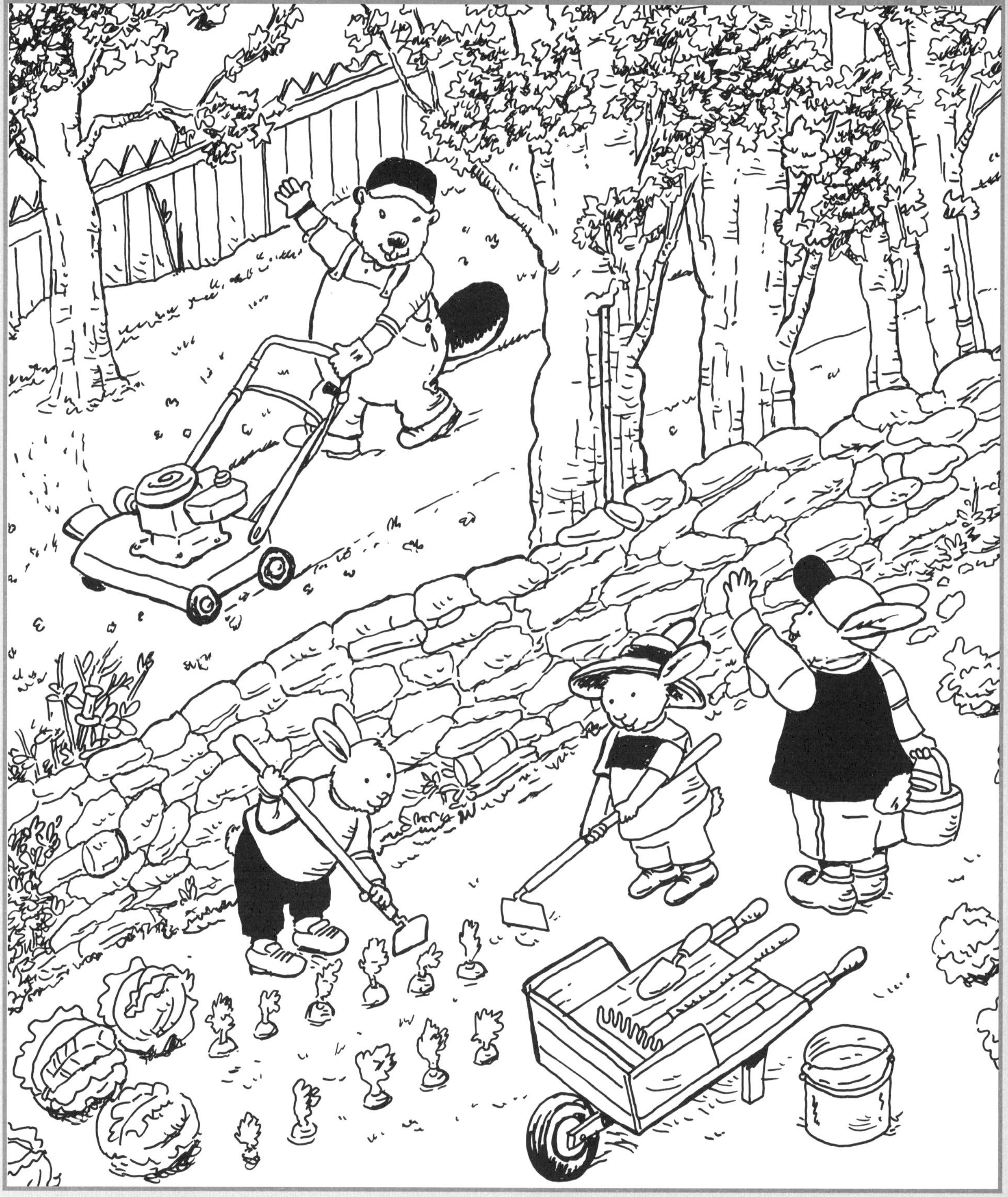

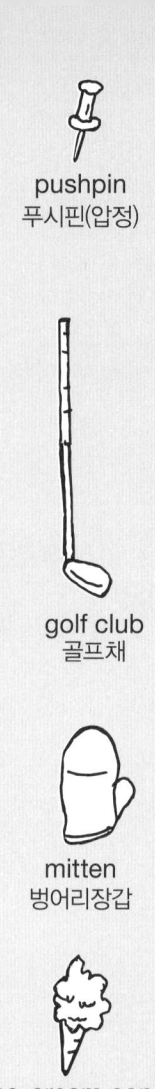

pushpin
푸시핀(압정)

golf club
골프채

mitten
벙어리장갑

ice-cream cone
아이스크림 콘

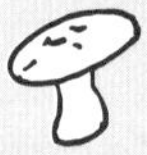
mushroom
버섯

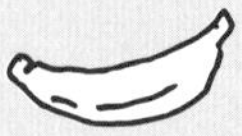
banana
바나나

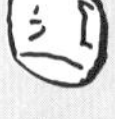
jar
병

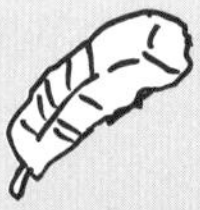
feather
깃털

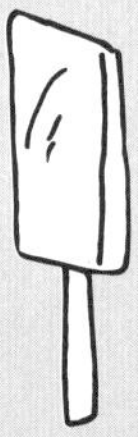
ice-cream bar
막대아이스크림

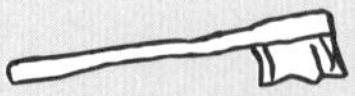
toothbrush
칫솔

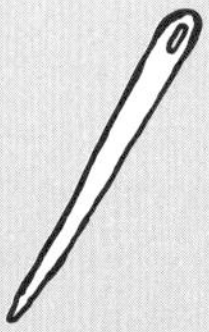
needle
바늘

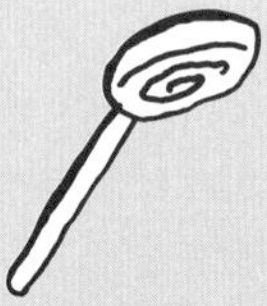
lollipop
막대사탕

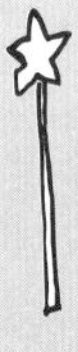
magic wand
마술 지팡이

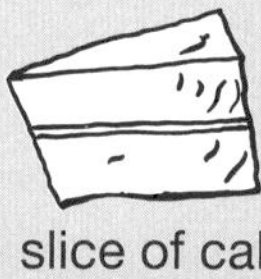
slice of cake
케이크 조각

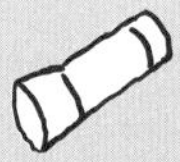
flashlight
손전등

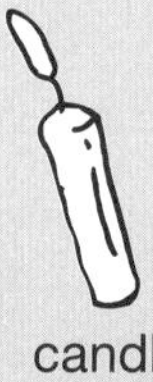
candle
양초

drumstick
북채

carrot
당근

slice of bread
빵 조각

banana
바나나

slice of pizza
피자 조각

wishbone
V자형 뼈

Streamside Cleanup 개울가 청소하기

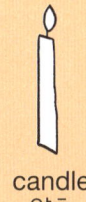
candle
양초

cherry
체리

apple
사과

toothbrush
칫솔

mushroom
버섯

muffin
머핀

Illustrated by Joe Wigfield

egg
계란

slice of pie
파이 조각

slice of bread
빵 조각

pencil
연필

sailboat
돛단배

crescent
moon
초승달

car
자동차

banana
바나나

fish
물고기

crown
왕관

heart
하트

saw
톱

shoe
신발

doll
인형

16 Highlights

snowman
눈사람

teacup
찻잔

comb
빗

pennant
삼각기

bell
종

feather
깃털

spider
거미

spoon
숟가락

eyeglasses
안경

snow cone
스노 콘
(시럽을 넣은
얼음과자)

paper clip
클립

toothbrush
칫솔

bird
새

Illustrated by Tim Davis

fan
부채

nail
못

handbell
핸드벨

screwdriver
드라이버

pennant
삼각기

open book
펴놓은 책

comb
빗

pencil
연필

hockey stick
하키 스틱

squirrel
다람쥐

rabbit
토끼

lizard
도마뱀

frog
개구리

kangaroo
캥거루

bicycle
자전거

sock
양말

sailboat
돛단배

cell phone
휴대전화

fork
포크

banana
바나나

Feeding the Fish 물고기에게 먹이주기

crescent moon
초승달

hammer
망치

heart
하트

teacup
찻잔

pen
만년필

book
책

Illustrated by Jennifer Emery

cherry
체리

ax
도끼

key
열쇠

wishbone
V자형 뼈

fishhook
낚싯바늘

plunger
플런저
(흡인식 하수관
청소기)

book
책

2 mushrooms
버섯 두 개

toothbrush
칫솔

flag
깃발

pencil
연필

banana
바나나

spatula
주걱

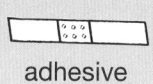
adhesive
bandage
반창고

dolphin
돌고래

ruler
자

wristwatch
손목시계

hanger
옷걸이

sailboat
돛단배

flag
깃발

teacup
찻잔

tube of
toothpaste
치약튜브

pushpin
푸시핀(압정)

olive
올리브

spoon
숟가락

spool of
thread
실패

caterpillar
애벌레

boot
부츠

Recorder Duet 리코더 듀엣 연주

Illustrated by Paul Richer

snow cone
스노 콘

ladder
사다리

fish
물고기

boot
부츠

fork
포크

mitten
벙어리장갑

seashell
조개껍질

broom
작은 비

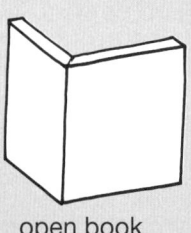

open book
펴놓은 책

scissors
가위

pencil
연필

banana
바나나

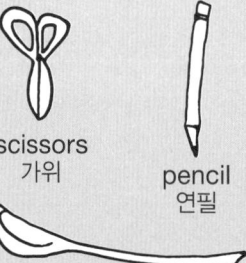

spoon
숟가락

slipper
슬리퍼

saucepan
냄비

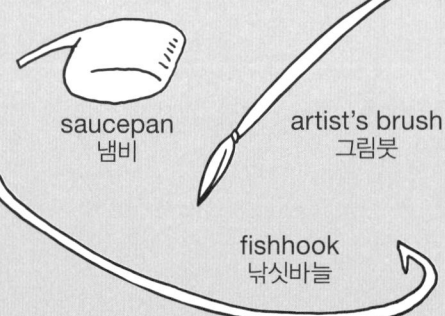

artist's brush
그림붓

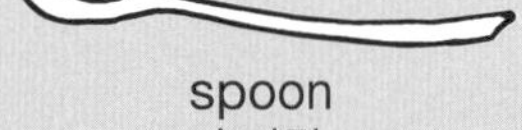

fishhook
낚싯바늘

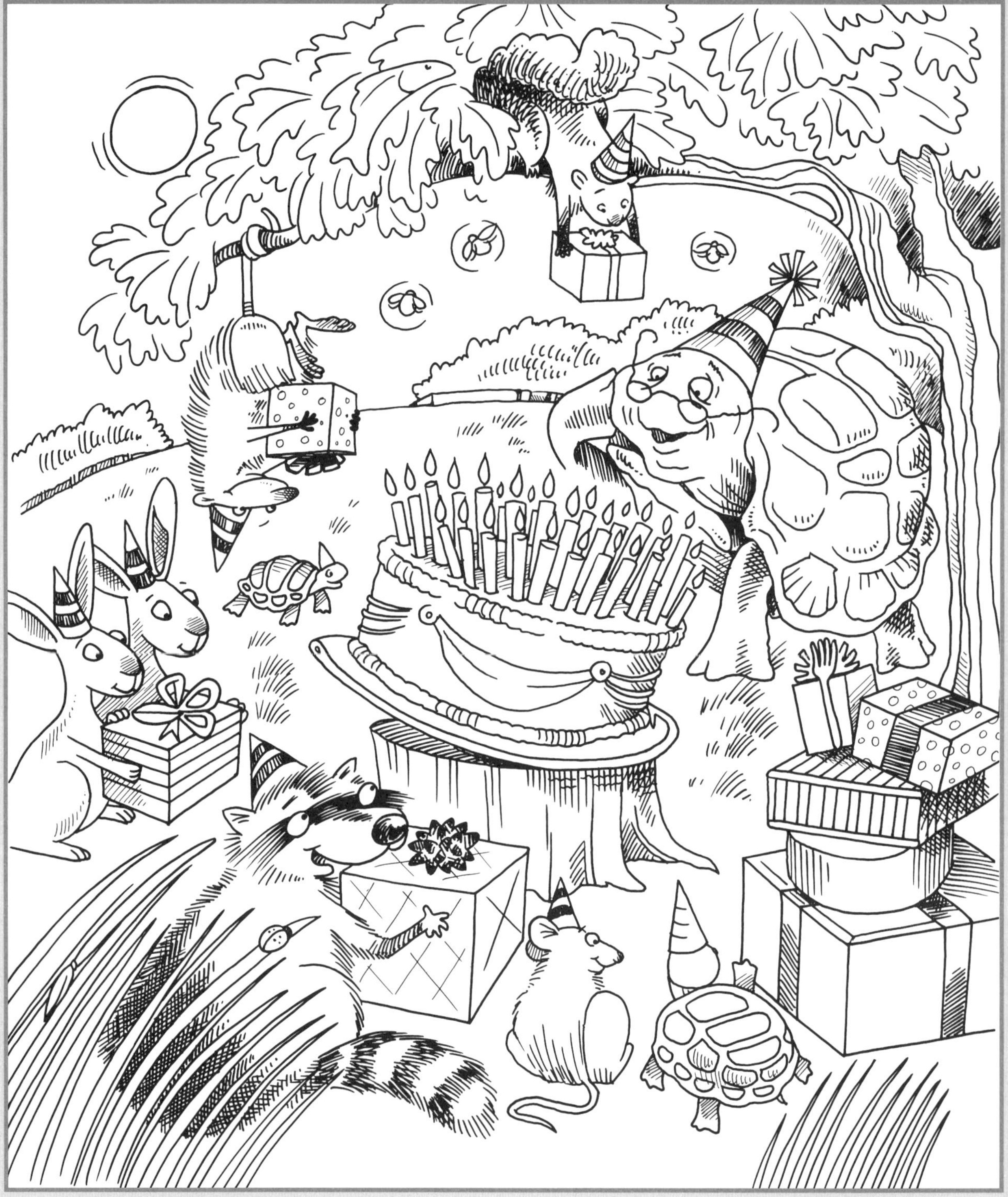

Illustrated by Karen Stormer Brooks

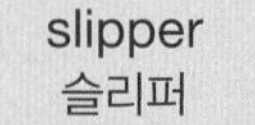

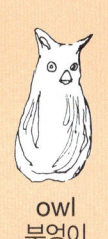

owl
부엉이

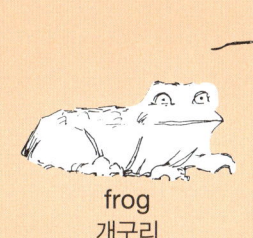

frog
개구리

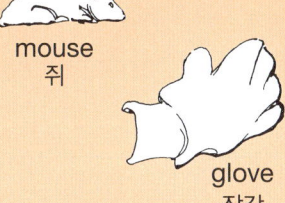

mouse
쥐

glove
장갑

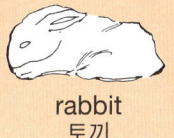

rabbit
토끼

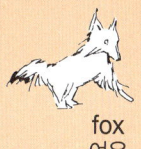

fox
여우

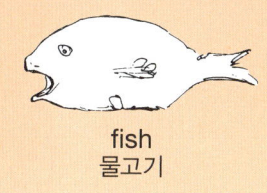

fish
물고기

Planting a Tree 나무 심기

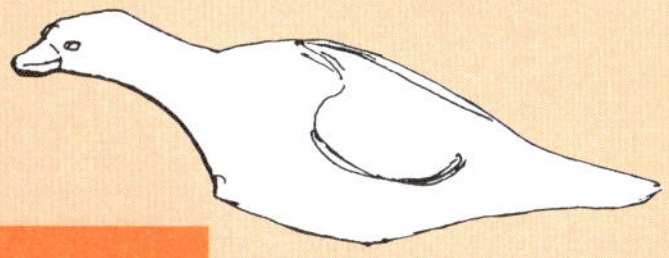

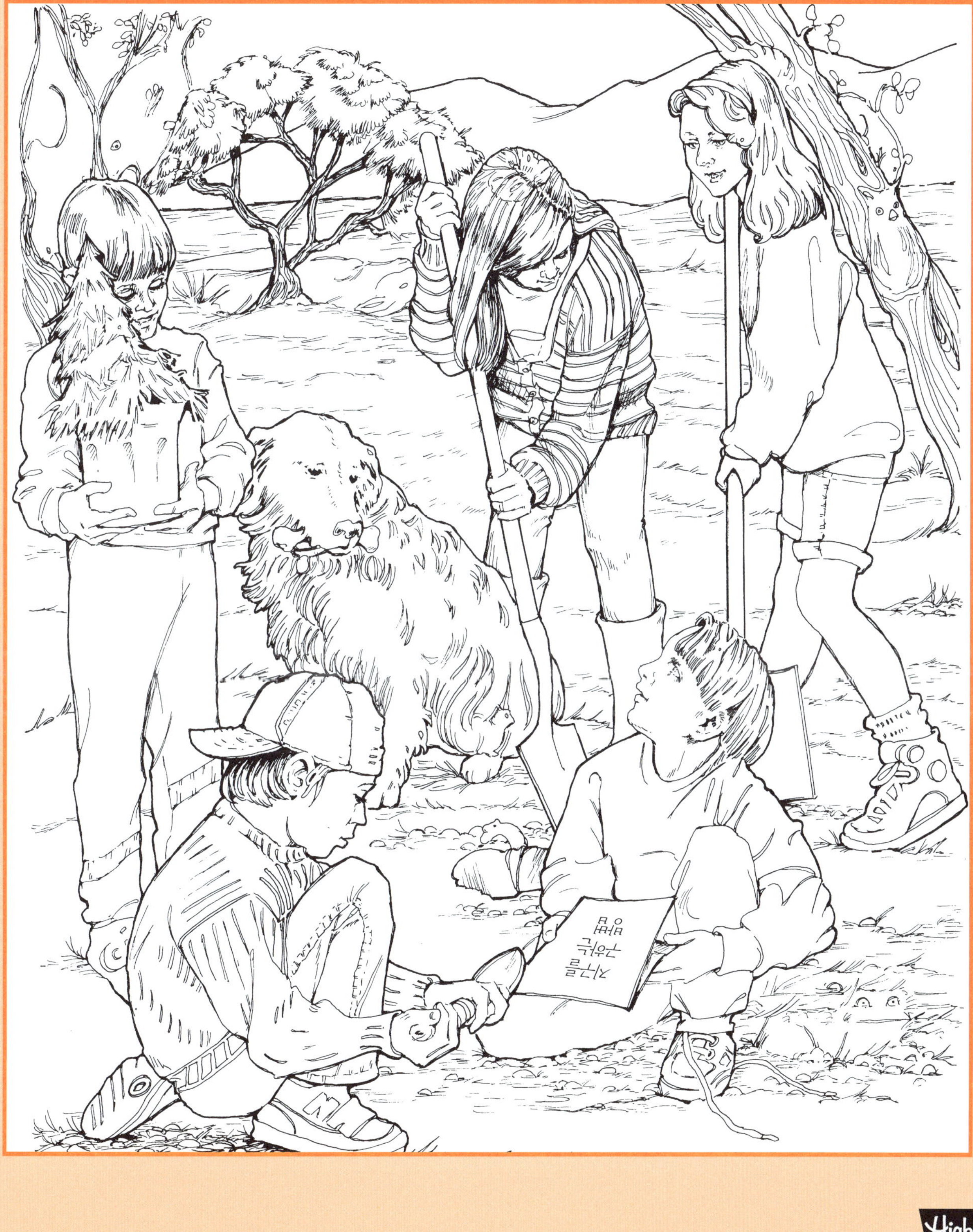

2 birds
새 두 마리

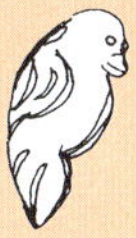

fork
포크

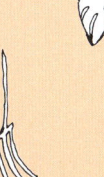

ladle
국자

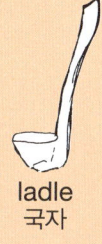

slice of pie
파이 조각

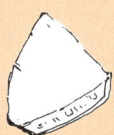

squirrel
다람쥐

ladder
사다리

butterfly
나비

Illustrated by Jodell Abrams

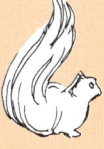

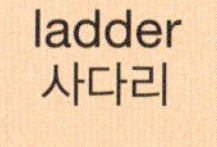

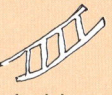

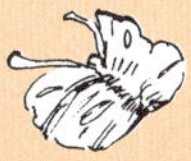

Look Who's Here 어, 이게 누구야!

mitten
벙어리장갑

heart
하트

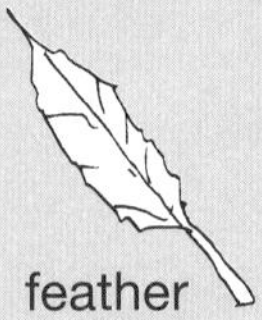

feather
깃털

candle
양초

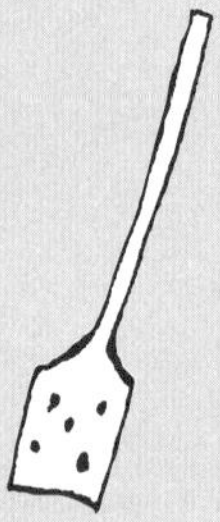

spatula
부침용 주걱

bird
새

nail
못

carrot
당근

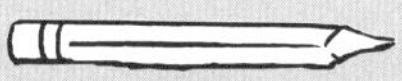

pencil
연필

artist's brush
그림붓

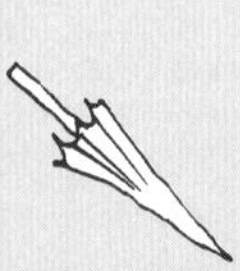

closed umbrella
접은 우산

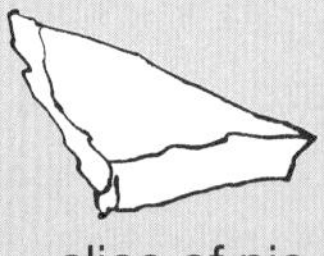

slice of pie
파이 조각

hamburger
햄버거

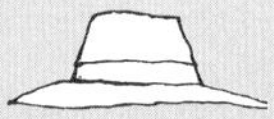

hat
모자

Illustrated by George Wildman

Highlights

yo-yo
요요

hoe
괭이

pencil
연필

spoon
숟가락

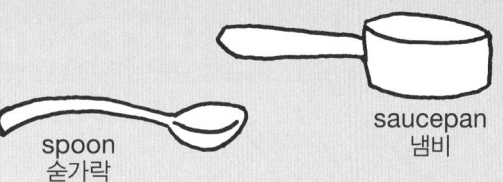
saucepan
냄비

ice-cream
cone
아이스크림 콘

Pottery Class 도자기 수업

shovel
삽

slice of pie
파이 조각

pushpin
푸시핀(압정)

butterfly
나비

musical note
음표

sailboat
돛단배

Illustrated by Charles Jordan

Highlights **25**

Dinnertime 저녁 식사 시간

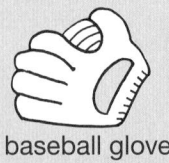

baseball glove
야구 장갑

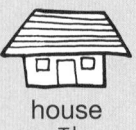

house
집

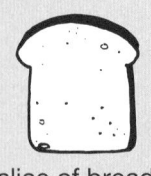

slice of bread
빵 조각

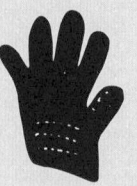

glove
장갑

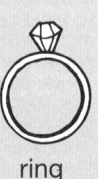

ring
반지

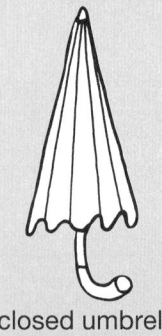

closed umbrella
접은 우산

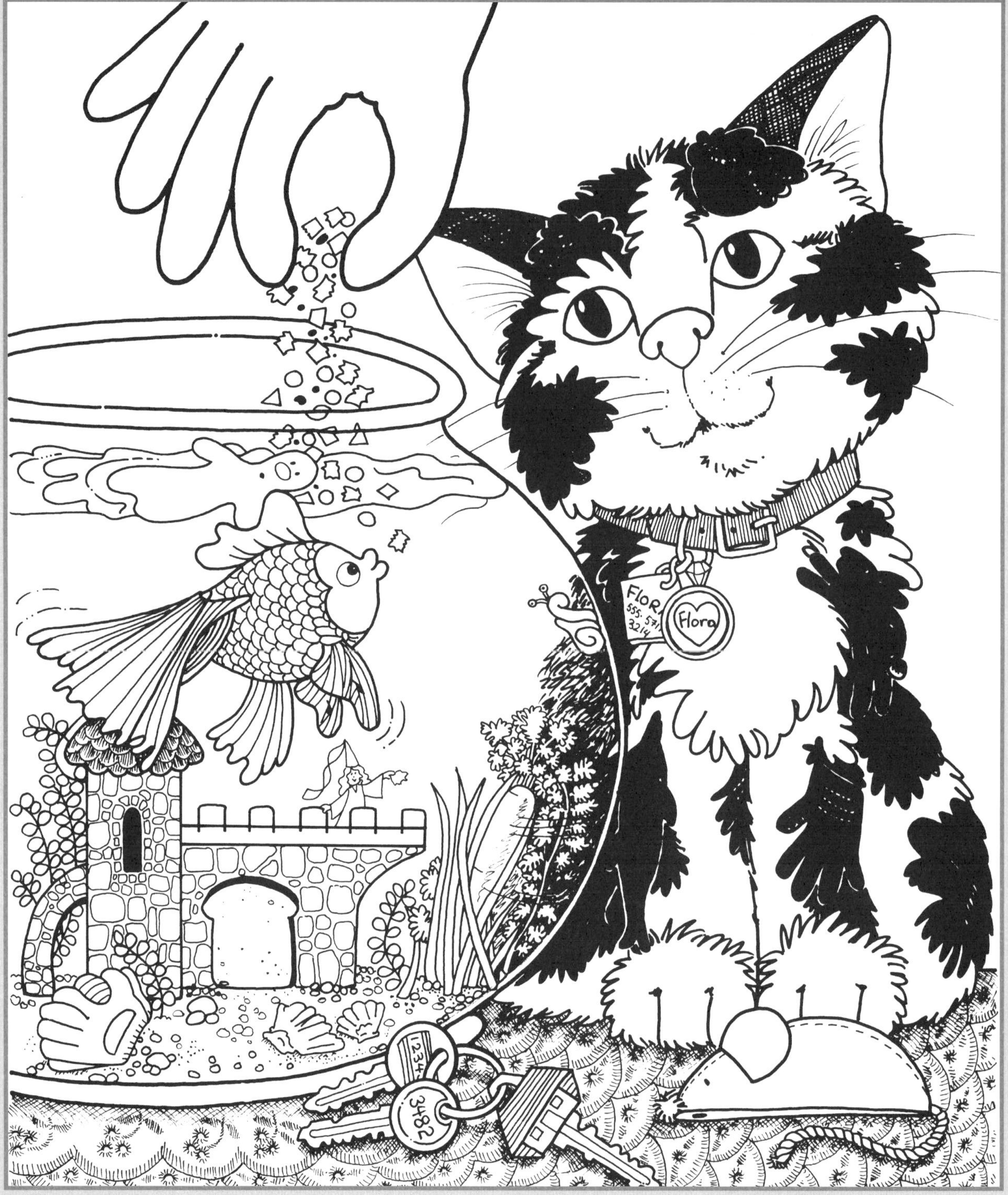

Illustrated by Susan T. Hall

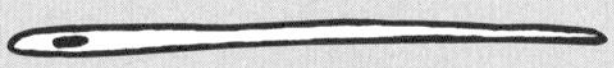

needle
바늘

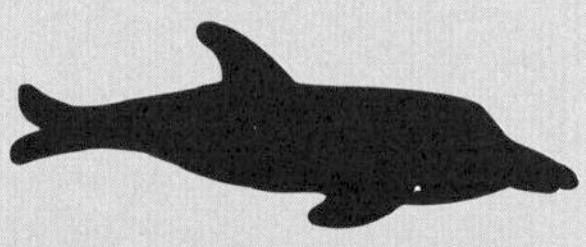

dolphin
돌고래

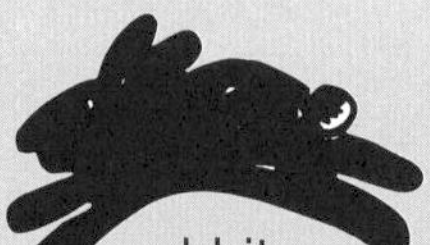

rabbit
토끼

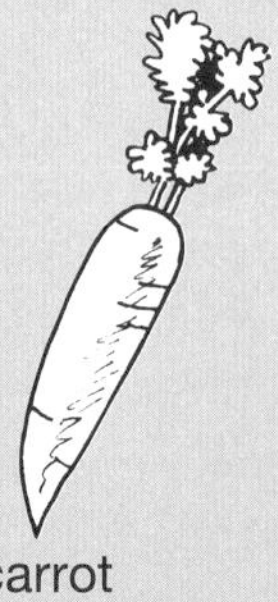

carrot
당근

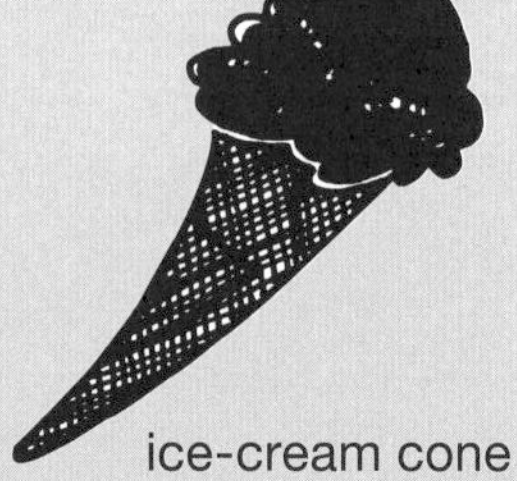

ice-cream cone
아이스크림 콘

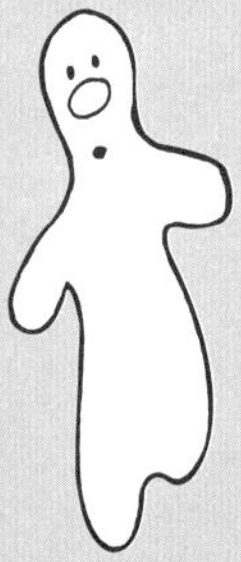

ghost
유령

artist's
brush
그림붓

book
책

pitcher
물주전자

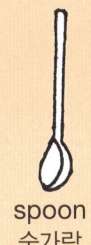
spoon
숟가락

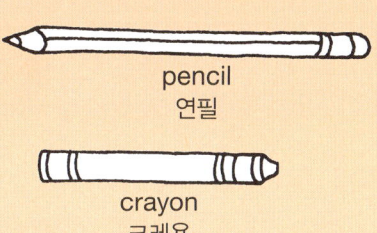
pencil
연필

crayon
크레용

lollipop
막대사탕

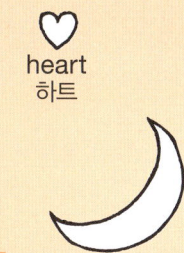
heart
하트

crescent moon
초승달

Sidewalk Fun 인도에서 놀기

Illustrated by Sally Springer

golf club
골프채

snake
뱀

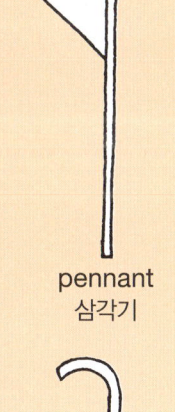
pennant
삼각기

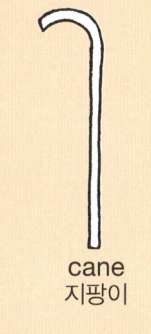
cane
지팡이

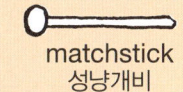
matchstick
성냥개비

모자

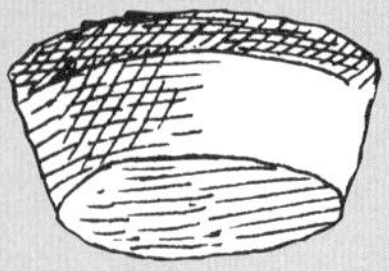

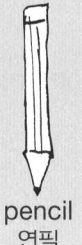

bowl
그릇

pencil
연필

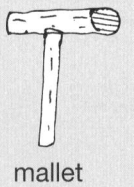

lamp
전등

mallet
나무망치

banana
바나나

screwdriver
드라이버

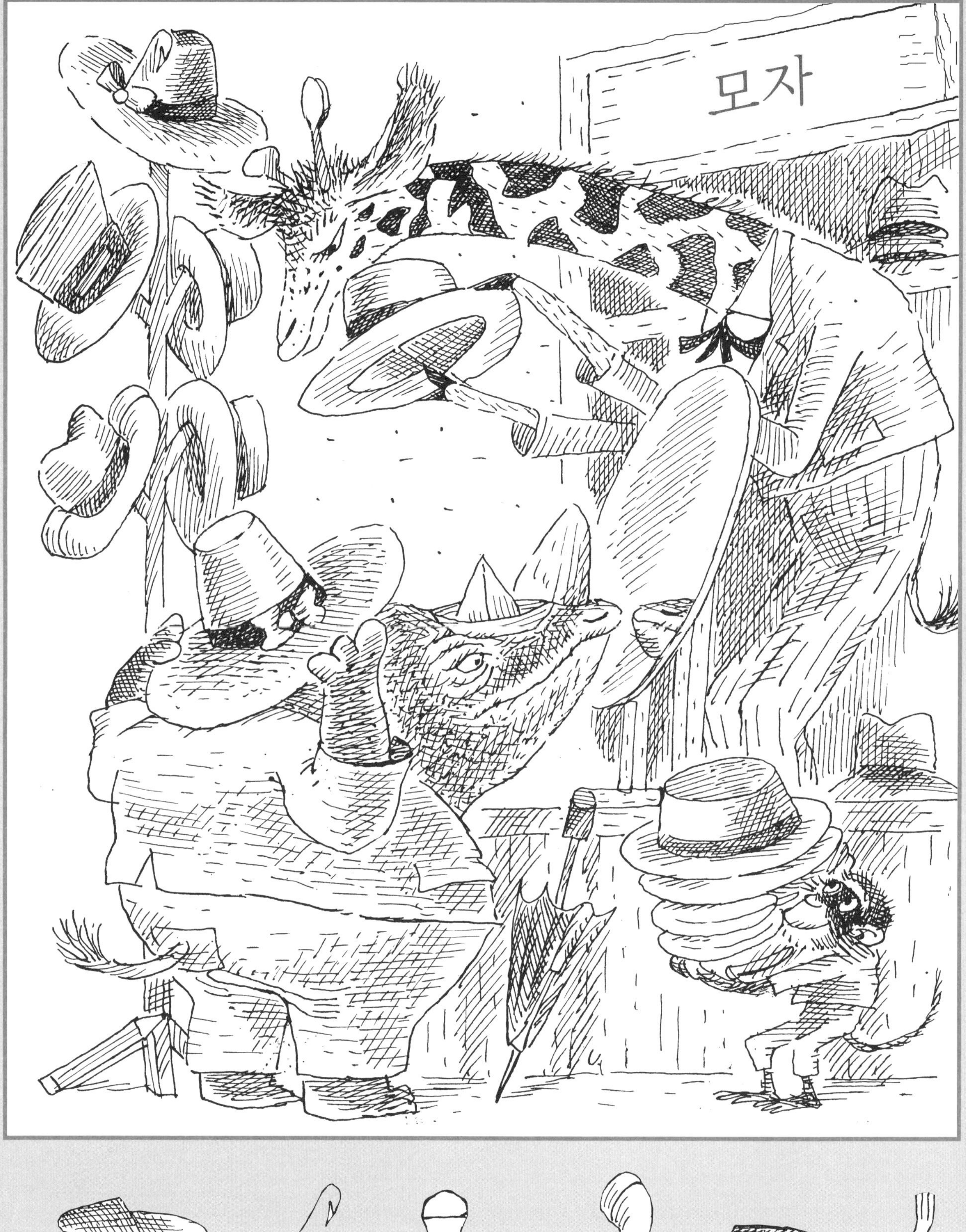

sailboat
돛단배

slipper
슬리퍼

spoon
숟가락

fishhook
낚싯바늘

ice-cream
cone
아이스크림 콘

telephone
receiver
전화 수화기

iron
다리미

fork
포크

Illustrated by Valeri Gorbachev

28 Highlights

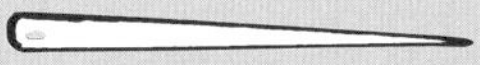

bird
새

hammer
망치

camera
카메라

needle
바늘

slice of pie
파이 조각

cat
고양이

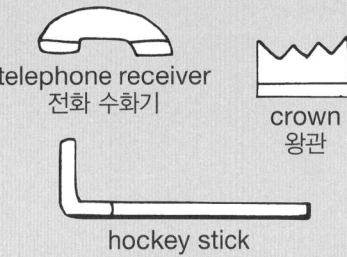
telephone receiver
전화 수화기

hockey stick
하키 스틱

crown
왕관

binoculars
쌍안경

shoe
신발

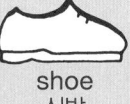

spatula
부침용 주걱

boomerang
부메랑

funnel
깔때기

slice of cake
케이크 조각

mushroom
버섯

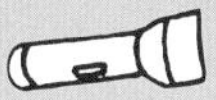

flashlight
손전등

paintbrush
페인트붓

At the Library 도서관에서 책 고르기

Illustrated by R. Michael Bn

Highlights **29**

The Bears Go Camping 곰들의 즐거운 캠핑

clothespin
빨래집게

ring
반지

tube of
toothpaste
치약튜브

ladle
국자

golf club
골프채

needle
바늘

screw
나사

artist's
brush
그림붓

lollipop
막대사탕

loaf of bread
빵 조각

fish
물고기

musical note
음표

flashlight
손전등

hammer
망치

wishbone
V자형 뼈

pen
만년필

bell
종

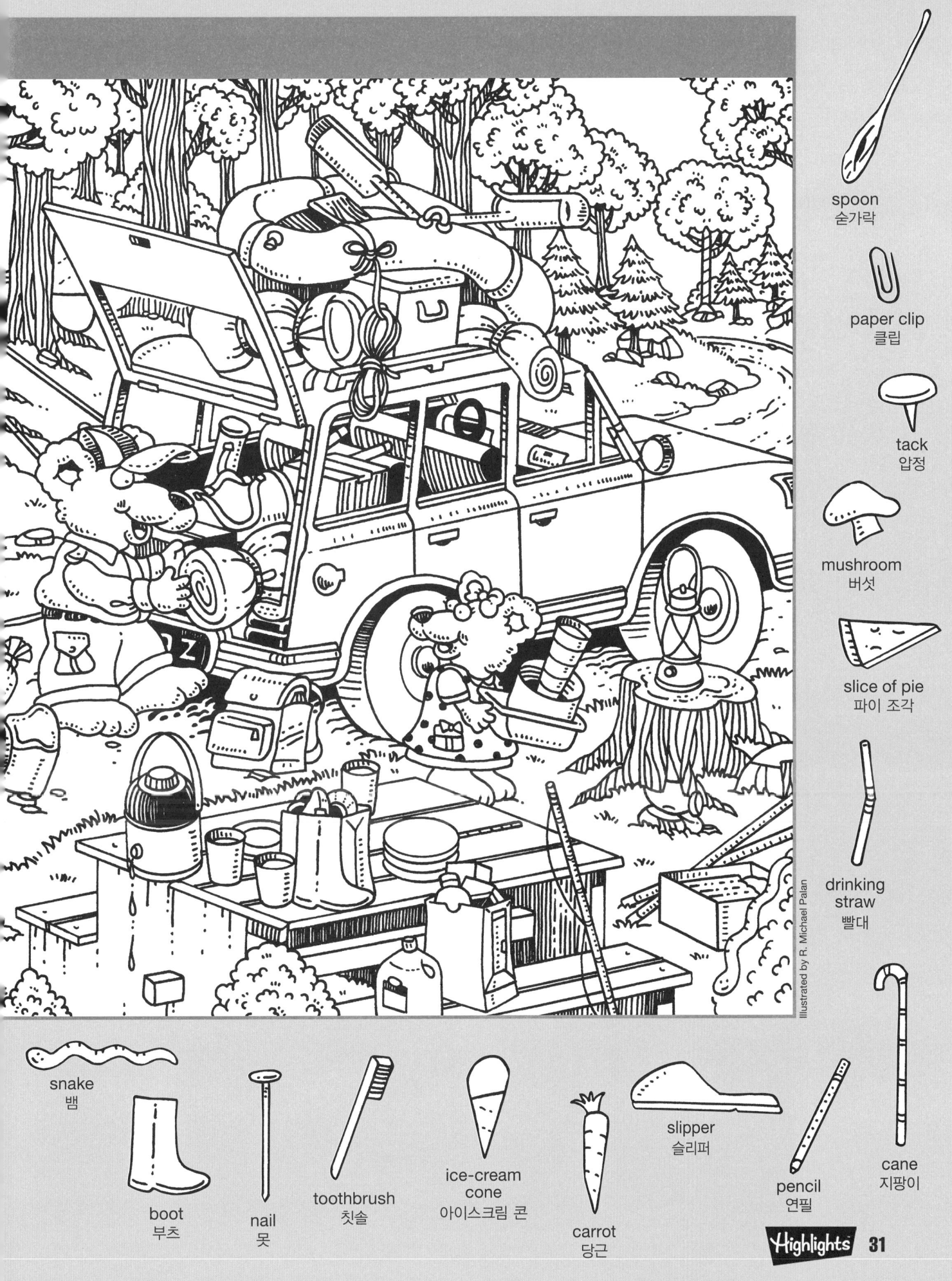

spoon
숟가락

paper clip
클립

tack
압정

mushroom
버섯

slice of pie
파이 조각

drinking
straw
빨대

cane
지팡이

Illustrated by R. Michael Palan

snake
뱀

boot
부츠

nail
못

toothbrush
칫솔

ice-cream
cone
아이스크림 콘

carrot
당근

slipper
슬리퍼

pencil
연필

It's Spring! 야, 봄이다!

spoon
숟가락

sailboat
돛단배

safety pin
안전핀

shuttlecock
셔틀콕
(배드민턴 경기에 쓰는 공)

umbrella
우산

heart
하트

birdhouse
새집

duck
오리

canoe
카누

horse's head
말의 머리

glove
장갑

bird
새

dog
개

telescope
망원경

Illustrated by Mij Colson-Barnum

Highlights

glove
장갑

football
럭비공

flashlight
손전등

snake
뱀

hot dog
핫도그

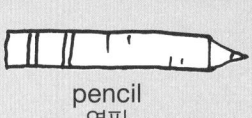
pencil
연필

banana
바나나

Washing the Car 즐겁게 세차하기

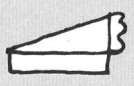
slice of pie
파이 조각

hamburger
햄버거

ice-cream
cone
아이스크림 콘

slice of bread
빵 조각

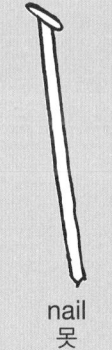
nail
못

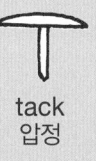
tack
압정

slice of pizza
피자 조각

Illustrated by Chuck Dillon

toothbrush
칫솔

sneaker
운동화

glove
장갑

tweezers
핀셋

light bulb
백열전구

pencil
연필

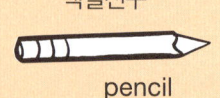

ice-cream bar
막대아이스크림

car
자동차

slice of pie
파이 조각

pine tree
소나무

button
단추

heart
하트

shoe
신발

bell
종

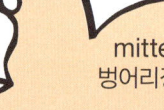

mitten
벙어리장갑

Highlights

Illustrated by Tim Davis

slice of pie
파이 조각

bell
종

screwdriver
드라이버

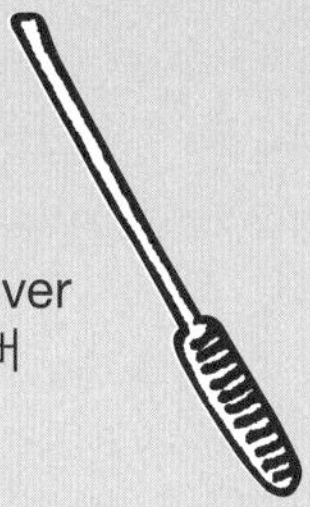

lollipop
막대사탕

ring
반지

canoe
카누

banana
바나나

ice-cream
cone
아이스크림 콘

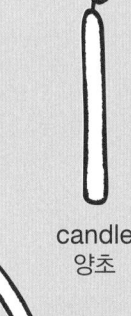
candle
양초

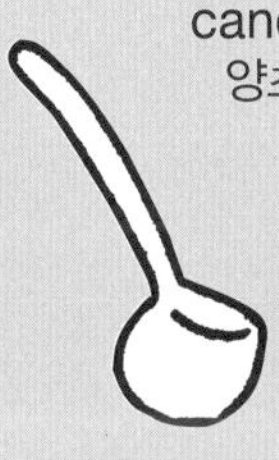

ladle
국자

tack
압정

feather
깃털

magnet
자석

Picnic in the Park 즐거운 공원 소풍

Illustrated by Ron Lieser

Highlights **35**

banana
바나나

goose
거위

sock
양말

mug
머그잔

carrot
당근

flute
플루트

flashlight
손전등

Grandpa's Roses 할아버지와 장미 심기

Illustrated by Elizabeth Allyn

wishbone
V자형 뼈

slice of pie
파이 조각

wedge of orange
오렌지 조각

handbell
핸드벨

mushroom
버섯

ladle
국자

measuring cup
계량컵

baseball cap
야구모자

ring
반지

eyeglasses
안경

baseball bat
야구방망이

closed
umbrella
접은 우산

ice-cream cone
아이스크림 콘

comb
빗

carrot
당근

turtle
거북

sock
양말

fishhook
낚싯바늘

paintbrush
페인트붓

magnifying
glass
돋보기

Illustrated by Viki Woodworth

38

toothbrush
칫솔

wedge of lemon
레몬 조각

mallet
나무망치

banana
바나나

bat
박쥐

paper clip
클립

worm
벌레

heart
하트

egg
계란

light bulb
백열전구

Engine 5 to the Rescue! 구조용 5번 자동차 출동!

2 bells
종 두 개

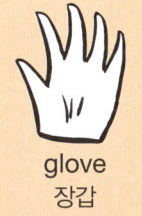

glove
장갑

magnifying glass
돋보기

crescent moon
초승달

crown
왕관

spoon
숟가락

Illustrated by Tim Davis

▼2~3페이지

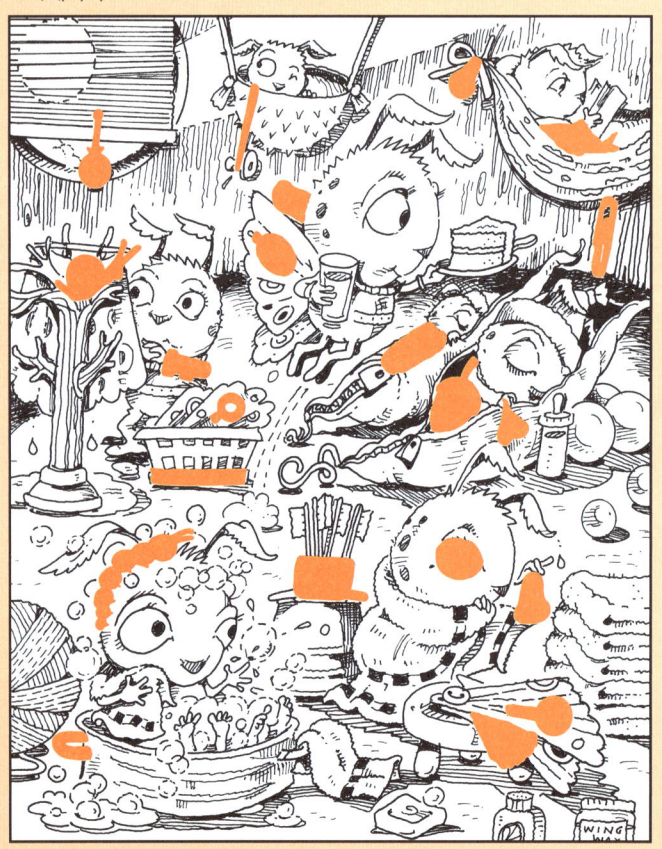

▼4페이지

▼5페이지

▼6페이지

▼7페이지

▼8페이지

▼9페이지

▼10페이지

▼11페이지

▼12페이지

▼13페이지

▼14페이지

▼15페이지

▼16~17페이지

정답

▼18페이지

▼19페이지

▼20페이지

▼21페이지

▼22페이지

▼23페이지

▼24페이지

▼25페이지

정답

▼26페이지

▼27페이지

▼28페이지

모자

▼29페이지

▼30~31페이지

▼32페이지

▼33페이지

▼34페이지

▼35페이지

▼36페이지

▼37페이지